500 Ways To Make Me Laugh Until I Cry!

Ticktock

An Hachette UK Company

www.hachette.co.uk

First published in the USA in 2014 by Ticktock,
an imprint of Octopus Publishing Group Ltd
Endeavour House
189 Shaftesbury Avenue
London
WC2H 8JY

www.octopusbooks.co.uk
www.octopusbooksusa.com
www.ticktockbooks.com

Copyright © Octopus Publishing Group Ltd 2014

Distributed in the US by
Hachette Book Group USA
237 Park Avenue
New York, NY 10017, USA

Distributed in Canada by
Canadian Manda Group
165 Dufferin Street
Toronto, Ontario, Canada M6K 3H6

All rights reserved. No part of this work may be reproduced or utilized in any form or by any means, electronic or mechanical, including photocopying, recording, or by any information storage and retrieval system, without the prior written permission of the publisher.

ISBN 978 1 78325 087 5

Printed and bound by CPI Group (UK) Ltd, Croydon, CR0 4YY

10 9 8 7 6 5 4 3 2 1

Text, illustration, and design: Duck Egg Blue
Project Editor: Mariangela Palazzi-Williams
Publisher: Samantha Sweeney
Managing Editor: Karen Rigden
Production Controller: Sarah Connelly
U.S. Editor: Jennifer Dixon

Every effort has been made to trace the copyright holders, and we apologize in advance for any unintentional omissions. We would be pleased to insert the appropriate acknowledgement in any subsequent edition of this publication.

THE END

Contents

Too Cool for School	6
Sporting Shenanigans	24
All Creatures Great and Small	34
Funny Folk	58
Kooky Dinners	75
It's a Crazy World	88
Planes, Trains, and Unicycles	99
Goofy Gadgets	109
Medical Madness	116
Monstrously Funny	127
Lunar Laughs	136

Too Cool for School

Mom: Time to get up and go to school!

Son: I don't want to go. Everyone hates me, and I get bullied!

Mom: But you have to go. You're the principal!

Why did the student throw his watch out of the classroom window?

He wanted to see time fly!

Mom: From now on, you are going to have free school lunches.

Son: But mom, I don't want three school lunches. One is more than enough!

RIDDLE

How do you make the number one disappear?

Add the letter "G" and it's "GONE"!

John: Great news! The teacher said we're going to have a test today, come rain or shine.

Sam: So, what's so great about that?

John: It's snowing!

Lunch lady: It's very rude to reach over the table for cookies. Have you lost your tongue?

Student: No, but my arms are longer!

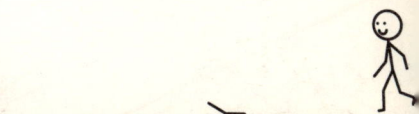

What do you get when you cross one principal with another?

I wouldn't do it - principals don't like to be crossed!

Why did the teacher go to the beach?

He wanted to test the water!

What's a teacher's favorite nation?

Expla-nation!

Why did the teacher wear sunglasses?

Because her class was so bright!

Why did the new boy steal a chair from the classroom?

Because the teacher told him to take a seat!

Why were the teacher's eyes crossed?

Because she couldn't control her pupils!

Why did the jelly bean go to school?

To become a smartie!

"My father gave me a really cheap dictionary for my birthday, but I couldn't find the words to thank him!"

Which hand is it better to write with?

Neither, you should use a pen!

Daughter: Dad, can you write in the dark?

Dad: I can try. What do you want me to write?

Daughter: Your signature on my report card!

Why have nursery school teachers got such a positive attitude?

They know how to make the little things count!

Teacher: I think you need glasses, Lewis.

Lewis: What makes you think that, Mr. Johnson?

Teacher: You're facing the wrong way!

Why does your teacher have her hair in a bun?

Because she has her nose in a burger!

Teacher: Emma, I wish you'd pay a little attention.

Emma: I'm paying as little as I can!

Teacher: Did your mom or dad help you with the questions?

Ryan: No, I got them wrong all by myself!

Teacher: Why did you bring eye shadow and lipstick to school, Eva? You know it is forbidden!

Eva: But miss, you told me I had to do a make-up test today because of the low mark I got yesterday!

Teacher: Which two words in English have the most letters?

Erin: Post office!

What happened to the plant when it went to its math lesson?

It grew square roots!

Dad: Holly, why is your test score so low?

Holly: Because of absence.

Dad: You were absent?

Holly: No, but the girl next to me was!

If a picture is worth a thousand words, then why shouldn't we judge a book by its cover?

What's a mushroom?

The place they store the school lunches!

Teacher: Did you know that most accidents happen in the kitchen?

Freddie: Yes, but we still have to eat them!

Why did the school cafeteria hire a dentist?

To make more filling meals!

Why was the broom late for school?

It overswept!

Teacher: Who invented King Arthur's round table?

Student: Was it Sir Cumference?

Is the new teacher strict?

I don't know. I'm too scared to ask!

RIDDLE

I usually wear a bright coat, have a black tip, and make marks wherever I go.
What am I?

A pencil!

I would tell you a joke about this blunt pencil, but it would be pointless.

Shelf 1:

- Slow Cooking! by Stu Pot
- Hidden Treasures in the Attic by Anne Teak
- THE TWELFTH MONTH by Dee Sember
- Magic Words by Abi Cadabra
- The Nervous Skydiver by Hugo First
- Good Luck! by Bess Twishes

Shelf 2:

- HOW TO BUILD A ROBOT by Anne Droid
- The Book of Rocks by G. Ology
- Just Say No! by Will Power
- How to Treat Insect Bites by Ivor Nitch
- Housework by Dustin Cook
- Ghosts, Ghouls, and Goblins by Emma Fraid

What did the pencil say to the protractor?

"Take me to your ruler!"

Teacher: Why are you doing your multiplication on the floor?

Max: You told me not to use tables!

Why did the teacher turn the lights on?

Because her class was so dim.

What's an inkling?

A baby fountain pen!

Why did the student take scissors to school?

He wanted to cut class!

Jess: Is the math teacher in a good mood today?

Freya: I wouldn't count on it!

Geography teacher: John, where is Turkey?

John: I have no idea, sir. I haven't seen it since Christmas!

I've always had a hard time with decimals - I just can't see the point!

Teacher: Ian, if you had 50 cents in one pocket and 70 cents in the other pocket, what would you have?

Ian: Somebody else's pants, miss.

END-OF-YEAR SCHOOL REPORT

Student: Bridget D. Fidget

Subject: Math

With grades like these, at least we know she doesn't cheat.

Subject: English

The improvement in Bridget's handwriting has revealed that she can't spell.

Subject: PE

Bridget has great speed, it's just a shame she runs in the wrong direction.

Subject: Music

I can only assume Bridget has an excellent ear for music as she's always listening to her mp3 player.

Subject: Geography

Bridget does well to find the classroom.

"I can accept a bad grade in most subjects, but an E in history?"

If teachers are so smart, how come their books have all the answers?

Geography teacher: Where's the Dead Sea?

Ewan: Dead? I never knew it was sick!

Geography teacher: Why did the explorers go to the South Pole?

Grace: To visit Aunt Arctica.

What happened when the wheel was invented?

It caused a revolution!

Knock, knock, who's there?
Norway.
Norway who?
Norway am I telling you any more knock, knock jokes!

Who invented fire?

Some bright spark!

Why does history keep repeating itself?

Because nobody was listening the first time around!

"Ben, were the pyramids built by the Ancient Egyptians?"

"I sphinx so sir!"

What kind of lunches do geometry teachers enjoy?

Square meals!

Did you hear about the math teacher whose mistakes started to multiply?

In the end, they had to take him away!

When I grow up, I want to be a...

- **POLICE OFFICER** Hans Cuffs
- **PLUMBER** Lee King
- **PRIVATE DETECTIVE** Ivor Clue
- **DENTIST** Phil McCavity
- **GEOLOGIST** Roxanne Minerals
- **ACCOUNTANT** Penny Pincher
- **LUMBERJACK** Tim Burr
- **LONG-DISTANCE TRUCK DRIVER** Miles Apart
- **FORTUNE TELLER** Claire Voyance

Sporting Shenanigans

Knock, Knock!
Who's there?
General Lee.
General Lee who?
Generally I go to practice, but today I've got a match!

How did the soccer field become a triangle?

Somebody took a corner!

Why is a doughnut like a golfer?

It has a hole in one!

RIDDLE

What can you serve, but not eat?

A tennis ball!

What do you call a pig who plays basketball?

A ball hog!

Why weren't the basketball players invited for dinner?

Because they dribbled too much!

Referee: William, I'm sending you off the football field!

William: What for?

Referee: The rest of the game!

What's the quietest sport?

Bowling – you can hear a pin drop!

What's a cat's favorite soccer kick?

A kitty-corner!

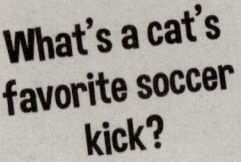

What do you call a very clever tennis player?

A racket scientist!

What goes putt-putt-putt-putt?

A bad golfer!

Why can't waiters play tennis?

They only want to serve!

Knock, Knock!
Who's there?
Caddy.
Caddy who?
Caddy your own clubs, pal!

How many golfers does it take to change a lightbulb?

Fore!

PLEASE DON'T PICK UP LOST BALLS UNTIL THEY STOP ROLLING!

"How's life?"

"Up and down!"

RIDDLE

What do you throw out when you want to use it, but take in when you don't want to use it?

A fishing line!

What musical instruments do Spanish fishermen play?

Cast-a-nets!

Why is a football stadium always cold?

Because it's full of fans!

"Coach, I've thought of a way to make the team better."

"Great! Are you leaving it?"

Why did the basketball player go to the doctor?

To get more shots!

Bad news guys. My doctor says I can't play baseball.

Really? When did he see you play?

RIDDLE

What is harder to catch the further you run?

Your breath!

Where do old bowling balls end up?

The gutter!

Why shouldn't you tell a joke while you're ice skating?

Because the ice might crack up!

What lights up a football stadium?

A football match!

What kinds of cats go bowling?

Alley cats!

Don't stop me. I'm on a roll!

> That man is so silly! He'll never catch that boat!

Knock, Knock!
Who's there?
Canoe.
Canoe who?
Canoe come out and play today?

What is a cheerleader's favorite color?

Yeller!

Prank #1

RIP-ROARING PANTS!

You will need: A piece of cloth and a water fountain.

Take a piece of old cloth with you to football or baseball practice, making sure you keep it well hidden.

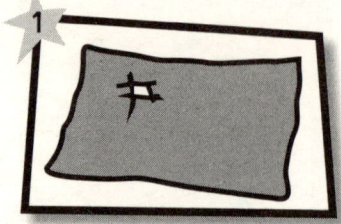

Follow your victim when they go to the water fountain. As they bend over to drink, tear the cloth to make a ripping sound.

Thinking that their pants have ripped, your victim will race back to the locker room, while you just watch and laugh!

PRANK LIKE A PRO: Select the right cloth and try out the ripping noise at home first – a piece of old cotton sheet is perfect.

"Look! The target is making an arrow escape!"

What happened when two balls of string had a race?

They ended up in a tie!

Two riders on a tandem bicycle reach the top of a steep hill, puffing and panting. "Phew, that was a hard climb," said the rider at the back. "You're not kidding," replied the rider at the front. "It's a good thing I kept the brakes on, or we would have slid back down the hill!"

All Creatures Great and Small

What does an oyster do on her birthday?

She shellebrates!

Where do sheep go to get their hair cut?

The baa baas!

What's the most musical fish?

The piano tuna!

How do toads greet one another?

"Wart's up?"

What did the snake say to his girlfriend after they had an argument?

"Let's hiss and make up!"

What kind of animal goes "oom"?

A cow walking backwards!

Where do turtles go when it rains?

To shell-ter!

What do birds watch on TV?

The feather forecast!

When does a cow get a bunch of flowers and breakfast in bed?

On M-udders Day!

How do rabbits keep their fur tidy?

With hare-spray!

What do you call a young goat that does martial arts?

The Karate Kid!

Why didn't the mussel have any friends?

Because he was a little shellfish!

What do cows play at birthday parties?

Moosical chairs!

Why did the tadpole feel lonely?

Because he was newt to the area!

What do you get when you cross a cow with a camel?

Lumpy milkshakes!

What's a skunk's favorite game in school?

Show and smell!

What do you call a sleeping bull?

A bulldozer!

What do you get when you cross an angry sheep with an angry cow?

An animal in a very baaaaaad moooood!

I love ewe!

What did the forgetful skunk say when the wind changed direction?

"It's all coming back to me now!"

Why was the little bear so spoiled?

Because its mother panda'd to its every whim!

Where do penguins vote?

At the South Poll!

Why did the skunk buy four boxes of tissues?

Because he had a stinking cold!

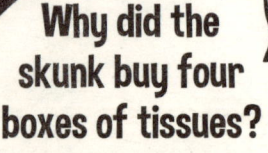

A snail entered a police station and told an officer, "I've just been mugged by two turtles. They beat me up and took all my money!" The officer replied, "Why, that's terrible. Did you get a good look at them?" "No sir, it all happened so fast!"

What's a skunk's philosophy of life?

Eat, stink, and be merry!

What did one slug say to the other?

"Slime flies when you're having fun!"

What did the farmer get when he crossed a centipede with a turkey?

100 drumsticks!

What happened to the leopard who took a bath three times a day?

After a week, he was spotless!

"Hey, long time no see!"

A man looks out his window and sees a snail on his best plant. He goes outside, picks up the snail, and throws him as far as he can. Two years later, the man hears a tap, tap, tap on his window. To his amazement, he sees the same snail, who looks right at him and asks, "What did you do that for?"

What did the hungry dalmatian say after his dinner?

"That hit the spots!"

RIDDLE

What has a baboon's bottom, a lion's mane, and a penguin's beak?

A zoo!

Why can't dalmatians play hide-and-seek?

They are always spotted!

Prank #2

A WILD ENCOUNTER!

You will need: A phone and the phone number of a local zoo or wildlife park.

Make a note of the phone number for the local zoo. Call your house number from your cell phone when your mom is busy and pretend to answer it.

Tell your mom that someone called Mr. Lyon called, and he asked if she could phone him back. Give her the number of the zoo and have a good giggle when she phones them asking to be put through to the king of the jungle!

PRANK LIKE A PRO: Make sure you pronounce "Lyon" as the animal, or the joke won't work.

What did the duck say when she bought some lipstick?

"Put it on my bill!"

What do you call a pig that does karate?

A pork chop!

RIDDLE

You are on a horse, galloping at a constant speed. You are surrounded by animals, all running in the same direction as you. Just behind you, there is a huge lion, which is running at the same speed as you. What can you do to escape this dangerous situation?

Get off the carousel!

What do you get if you cross a chicken with a cement mixer?

A bricklayer!

Where do you buy baby birds?

At the chickout!

What is the quietest kind of dog?

A hush puppy!

What do whales eat?

Fish and ships!

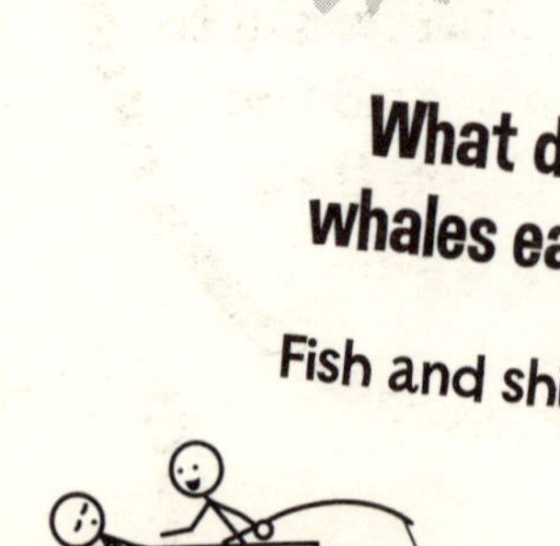

Why did the duck cross the road?

To prove he wasn't a chicken!

What bird is with you at every meal?

A swallow!

What do you call a bird in the winter?

Brrr-d!

Knock, Knock!
Who's there?
Kook!
Kook who?
Don't call me cuckoo!

Boy: I'd like to buy some birdseed.

Shop assistant: OK. How many birds do you have?

Boy: None! I want to grow some!

A man was driving along a road with three penguins in his car. A policeman signalled for him to pull over. "Why have you got three penguins in your car? You must take them to the zoo," he said. The next day, the policeman saw the man again. He still had the penguins in the back of his car. "Hey, I thought I told you yesterday to take those penguins to the zoo," said the officer. "I did," said the man, "and they loved it! Today I'm taking them to the beach!"

There were two cows in a field. The first cow said "Moo" and the second cow said "Baaaa." "Why did you say 'baaaa'?" the first cow asked the second cow. "I'm learning a foreign language," the second cow replied.

What should you do if your dog chews a dictionary?

Take the words out of his mouth!

How does a mouse feel after it takes a shower?

Squeaky clean!

What did one firefly say to the other?

"I've got to glow now!"

What do you call 100 spiders on a tire?

A spinning wheel!

Why was the baby ant confused?

Because all his uncles were ants!

What do you call a thieving alligator?

A crookodile!

What do you get if you cross a firefly and a moth?

An insect that can see its way around a dark closet!

What do you call a fly without wings?

A walk!

Who is a bee's favorite painter?

Pablo Beecasso!

What has antlers and sucks blood?

A moose-quito!

What's even smarter than a talking bird?

A spelling bee!

"Here comes the 9:45!"

Why did the spider take her laptop to the beach?

So she could surf the web!

What do you get if you cross a centipede and a parrot?

A walkie-talkie!

Why don't centipedes play soccer?

It takes too long to put their cleats on!

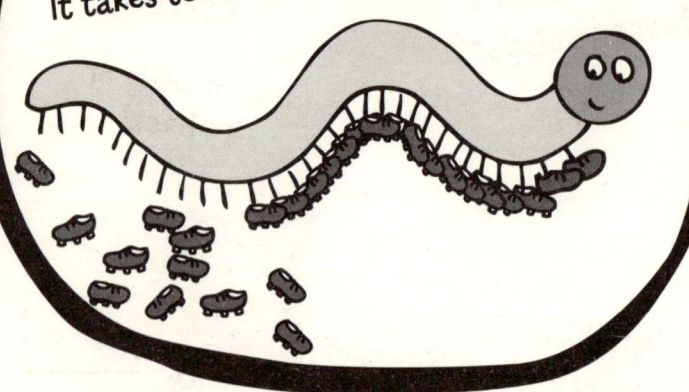

Why did the firefly keep stealing things?

He was light-fingered!

What did one girl firefly say to the other?

You glow girl!

What's a spider's favorite meal?

Corn on the cobweb!

Who is a bee's favorite singer?

Sting!

What is both on the ground and a hundred feet in the air?

A centipede on its back!

What do moths study in school?

Mothematics!

Did you hear about the caterpillars that got married?

It was larva at first sight!

What do you call a bug that can't have too much sugar?

A diabeetle!

What does a spider do when he gets angry?

He goes up the wall!

What kind of gas do snails buy?

Shell!

He's so cute. You must be so proud!

What do you call two spiders that just got married?

Newly webs!

What lives in gum trees?

Stick insects!

When do spiders go on their honeymoon?

After their webbing day!

What do polar bears eat for lunch?

Ice-bergers!

What kinds of bugs live in clocks?

Ticks!

What do fireflies eat?

Light snacks!

Prank #3
ICE-COLD BUGS!

You will need: Small fake bugs from a joke or toy shop and an ice cube tray.

Place a fake bug in each compartment of the ice tray. Fill the ice tray with water and freeze.

When someone asks for ice, put the bug-filled ice cubes in their glass and watch as they freak out!

PRANK LIKE A PRO: Choose the right moment for maximum effect. A party or a family celebration is the perfect occasion to share a good practical joke and have a laugh together!

What did one bee say to the other bee on a sunny day?

"Swarm today, isn't it?"

Who is a bee's favorite pop group?

The bee gees!

What's a bee-line?

The shortest distance between two buzz-stops!

Funny Folk

What do you call the child of parents from Iceland and Cuba?

An ice cube!

Girl, talking to her brother: "I didn't recognize you for a moment. It was one of the happiest moments in my life!"

Hey, little sis, why did you tell everyone at school I am an idiot?

Sorry, I didn't know it was a secret!

"Dad, does money grow on trees?"

"Of course not, darling."

"Then why do banks have branches?"

How do you know that carrots are good for your eyesight?

Have you ever seen a rabbit wearing glasses?

Little Susie complained, "Mom, my tummy aches." "That's because your tummy is empty," her mother replied. "You would feel better if you had something in it." That evening her father complained that he had a headache. "That's because it's empty," Susie said. "You'd feel better if you had something in it!"

"What's your father's occupation?" asked the teacher on the first day of school. "He's a magician, miss," answered the new boy. "He saws people in half." "Gosh!" replied the teacher. "Do you have any brothers or sisters?" "One half-brother and two half-sisters!"

I've got a good idea!

Must be beginner's luck!

Bobby: Katie, why are you taking that pencil to bed?

Katie: To draw the curtains, silly!

Prank #4

CRAZY TIME TURNER!

You will need: As many watches, alarm clocks, and clocks as you can find.

When nobody is looking, change the time forward by at least an hour on all the clocks in the house. Keep your watch unchanged, so that you know what the actual time is.

We're late!

Watch your victims run around like headless chickens trying to work out the time while getting ready for their meeting. Keep a safe distance... they will be very annoyed!

PRANK LIKE A PRO: Don't be cruel. Give them plenty of time to get to their appointment!

"I've changed my mind."

"Finally! Does the new one work any better?"

What's the best present ever?

A broken drum. You can't beat that!

Mother: Are you talking back to me?

Son: Well, yeah, that's how communication works.

What did the talking weight machine say when Auntie Maureen stepped on it?

"One at a time, please!"

A mother takes her son to buy a pair of school shoes. As he tries them on, the shop assistant asks, "How do they feel?" "The right one feels a bit tight," the boy replies. "Oh, but you have to try it with the tongue out!" The boy looks at her and replies "Thorry, it thill feelth a bit thight!"

What's a baby's motto?

If at first you don't succeed, cry, cry, and cry again!

Mom's cooking is improving! The smoke isn't as black as it used to be!

Prank #5

A ZESTY DRINK!

You will need: Two plastic bottles, water, and some clear vinegar.

Fill a couple of plastic water bottles with water. Add a few drops of vinegar to one of them and then put them both in the fridge. Convince your victim to go for a jog or a long bike ride and take the bottles with you.

When you stop for a break, start drinking from your bottle. Offer the other one to your victim, then take cover as they spit out the contents!

PRANK LIKE A PRO: Use bottles with different colored tops to make sure you don't get them mixed up. And carry an extra bottle of clean water for your victim: they'll need it!

Dad: John, would you like a pocket calculator for Christmas?

Son: No, dad. I already know how many pockets I have, thanks!

Mother: William, you've put your shoes on the wrong feet!

William: But these are the only feet I've got!

RIDDLE

Mark's mom has four children. The first is called April, the second is called May, and the third is called June. What's the fourth called?

ıMark!

What happened to the granny who put her false teeth in backwards?

She ate herself!

"I used to work with thousands under me!" grandpa said to his wide-eyed grandchildren. "Really? Where did you work?" one of them asked. "At the cemetery," replied grandpa.

My gran was a medium.

Interesting. Mine was a large!

What do you call...

What do you call a girl with a frog on her head?

Lily!

What do you call a girl across a river?

Bridget!

What do you call a boy with a shovel on his head?

Doug!

What do you call a girl with a cash register on her head?

Tilly!

What do you call a boy on your doorstep?

Matt!

A guard asked a prisoner what he was in jail for. "Doing my Christmas shopping early," replied the man. "That doesn't seem a crime to me!" replied the officer. "It is if the shops haven't opened yet!"

Why are pirate flags always in a bad mood?

Because they have crossbones!

What do you call an underwater spy?

James Pond!

What did the pirate name his daughter?

Peggy!

One day a mailman was greeted by a boy and a huge dog. The mailman asked the boy, "Does your dog bite?" "No," replied the boy. Just then the dog bit the mailman. The man yelled, "I thought you said your dog doesn't bite!" "I did" replied the boy. "But that's not my dog!"

Mailman 1: A dog bit me on the leg this morning.

Mailman 2: Did you put anything on it?

Mailman 1: No, he liked it plain.

Why does it take pirates so long to learn the alphabet?

Because they spend years at C!

How much did the pirate pay for his hook and peg leg?

An arm and a leg!

What do you get if you cross a painter with a policeman?

A brush with the law!

A police recruit was asked during the exam, "What would you do if you had to arrest your own mother?"

"Call for backup," he answered.

What do you call people who are afraid of Santa Claus?

Claus-trophobic!

What did the lawyer name his daughter?

Sue!

Why did the book join the police force?

It wanted to go undercover!

Why did the tap dancer retire?

He kept falling into the sink!

An armed robber went into a bank and shouted, "Gimme all your money or you're geography!" "Er," said the stunned teller, "don't you mean history?" "Shut up," shouted the robber, "and don't change the subject!"

What happened to the robber who stole a bar of soap?

He made a clean getaway!

Did you hear about the identical twins who robbed a bank?

After they were caught, they finished each other's sentences!

How did the grave digger get his job?

He just fell into it!

Did you hear about the man who bought a paper shop?

It folded!

What is an archaeologist?

Someone whose career is in ruins!

Did you hear about the two little boys who found themselves in a modern art gallery? "Quick," said one, "Run, before they say we did it!"

Why did the handyman have to get false teeth?

He kept biting his nails!

What should you wear when your basement is flooded?

Pumps!

Why did the clown wear loud socks?

So his feet wouldn't fall asleep!

What kind of training do you need to be a garbage collector?

None – you just pick it up as you go along!

Kooky Dinners

Why did the cookie cry?

Because its mom had been a wafer so long!

Why did the carrot look down the toilet?

He wondered where the peas had gone!

RIDDLE

What is black when you buy it, red when you use it, and gray when you throw it away?

Charcoal!

What are the worst vegetables to serve on a boat?

Leeks!

Customer: Excuse me, waiter. Will my pizza be long?

Waiter: Er, no sir, it'll be round!

How do you make an onion giggle?

Pickle it!

How do you fix a broken pizza?

With tomato paste!

RIDDLE

You throw away the outside and cook the inside. Then you eat the outside and throw away the inside. What is it?

An ear of corn!

Did you hear about the strawberry who went to charm school?

He became a real smoothie!

What's the opposite of a somersault?

A winter pepper!

Prank #6

JELLIED JUICE!

You will need: Plastic cups, straws, and some raspberry jello powder.

Dissolve the jello powder in hot water, following the instructions on the packet.

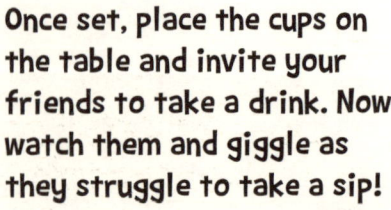

Place a straw in each plastic cup and pour in the jello while it's still liquid. Place in the fridge for a few hours to set.

Once set, place the cups on the table and invite your friends to take a drink. Now watch them and giggle as they struggle to take a sip!

PRANK LIKE A PRO: Prepare a normal raspberry drink for yourself and start drinking it before everybody else. Make sure you hold down the straw so that they don't notice the difference with their drink.

What did one strawberry say to the other?

"Look at the jam you've got us into!"

Why are chefs mean?

They beat eggs, whip cream, and mash potatoes!

What do you call an overweight pumpkin?

Plumpkin!

Why did the apple go out with a fig?

It couldn't find a date!

How do you start a jello race?

Get set!

Knock, Knock!

Who's there?

Figs.

Figs who?

Figs the doorbell, it's broken!

What do you call a lazy baker?

A loafer!

"Waiter, is there soup on the menu?"

"No, sir. I wiped it off!"

"Waiter, do you serve crabs?"

"Of course, sir. We serve anybody!"

What did one plate say to the other plate?

"Lunch is on me!"

Why was the chef so relaxed?

He had plenty of thyme on his hands!

What animal is like a yogurt?

A moose!

What did the nut say when it sneezed?

"A cashew!"

"Waiter, can I have my lunch on the patio?"

"Certainly, sir, but most people prefer to have it on the plate!"

I thought you were on a seafood diet?

I am. When I see food, I eat it!

Why couldn't the teddy bear eat his food?

Because he was stuffed!

"I got food poisoning from dinosaur meat the other day. I ate it ROAR!"

What did the oil and vinegar say when someone opened the kitchen cabinet door?

"Close the door, we're dressing!"

What's the best thing to put into a pie?

Your teeth!

What do garbage collectors eat?

Junk food!

Knock, Knock!
Who's there?
Justin!
Justin who?
Justin time for lunch!

What do snowmen like to eat for breakfast?

Frosted flakes!

I always talk to my food before I eat. It's the only way I can be sure it will agree with me.

Why couldn't the Christmas turkey escape the roasting pan?

He was foiled!

Prank #7

FROZEN BREAKFAST!

You will need: A bowl, milk, cereal, and a freezer.

Pour some milk in the bowl and add your victim's favorite cereal.

Place the bowl of milk and cereal in the freezer and leave it overnight.

The next morning, offer to prepare breakfast. Place the frozen cereal and a spoon in front of your victim and watch them as they try to eat their breakfast!

PRANK LIKE A PRO: To make your serving more realistic, top it up at the last minute with some fresh milk and a sprinkle of cereal.

It's a Crazy World

> It's lovely, but why did they build the castle so close to the airport?

What did the envelope say to the stamp?

"Stick with me, and we'll go places!"

What do penguins do on vacation?

Chill!

Where do pianists go on vacation?

The Florida Keys!

Why did the dalmatian take so long to choose his vacation?

He was looking for the right spot!

What do you call a manmade vacation island?

Con-Crete!

Where do cows go on vacation?

Moo York!

A businessman was struggling to carry his lumpy, oversized bag onto the plane. Helped by a flight attendant, he finally managed to stuff it into the overhead compartment. "Do you always carry such heavy luggage?" she sighed. "This is the last time" the man said. "Next time, I'm going in the bag and my wife can buy the ticket!"

Sorry, I couldn't book our vacation because the sign in the window at the travel agent said "GO AWAY!"

What do you call a passenger covered in salt and pepper?

A seasoned traveller!

A Scotsman visiting London was checking out of his hotel. "And how was your stay, sir?" asked the receptionist as he paid the bill. "Terrible!" he said. "At four o'clock this morning there was so much banging. Banging on the walls, banging on the door - even banging on the ceiling. It was so loud I could hardly hear myself playing the bagpipes!"

Prank #8

HIDDEN SURPRISE!

You will need: A beach towel and a shovel.

While at the beach, convince your victim to go and get an ice cream. When they're out of sight, remove their beach towel and start digging a hole in the sand, then remove all evidence of the sand you've dug up.

Replace the towel making sure it covers the hole and is flat on the ground. Then wait for your victim to return and invite him or her to sit down and enjoy their ice cream!

PRANK LIKE A PRO: Don't make the hole too deep or too wide – a little dent in the sand is enough for them to sink in!

A guide is showing a group of tourists around a castle. "Nothing has changed - not a stone has been touched in over 500 years," he explained. "Really?" said one of the tourists. "We must have the same landlord!"

What do you get when you throw a million books into the ocean?

A title wave!

A young man turns up at a hotel. "I'd like a single room, please," he asks. "Certainly, sir," says the receptionist. "With bath or shower?" The man doesn't have much money, so he asks, "What's the difference?" "You have to stand in the shower," replies the receptionist.

What do you call six weeks of rain in Scotland?

Summer!

What's the biggest problem with snow boots?

They melt!

How do you dress in Sweden during winter?

What did one Arctic explorer say to the other Arctic explorer?

"I'd hate to have a bear behind in this weather!"

Quickly!

What is the fastest country in the world?

Russia!

Why is Britain the wettest country?

Because royalty has reigned there for years!

Prank #9

SHORT SHEETS!

You will need: A bed made with sheets and blankets.

Take all the bedding off the bed, leaving the bottom sheet on the mattress.

Lay the top sheet on the bed, so that the end that is usually at the pillow end is at the bottom. If there's a pattern on the sheet, make sure it's facing down.

Tuck the top sheet under the mattress at the pillow end and fold the sheet in half so that the bottom edge is now at the pillow end, too.

Replace the blanket and fold the top edge of the sheet over it. Tuck in the edges and return the pillow to the bed. When your victim goes to bed, they'll find that they can't get in properly!

PRANK LIKE A PRO: Cover your tracks by making sure the bed is neatly made.

Reg wondered why the boomerang kept getting bigger until, all of a sudden, it hit him.

What should you take on a trip to the desert?

A thirst-aid kit!

Where can you find an ocean with no water?

On a map!

HEY!

A man arrived at a hotel where he had made a reservation rather late at night. All the lights were out, so he knocked on the door. After a long time, a light appeared in an upstairs window, and a woman called out, "Who are you? What do you want?" "I'm staying here!" the man replied. "Well, stay there, then," she shouted, and slammed the window shut.

What type of rocks are never found in the ocean?

Dry ones!

What did one campfire say to the other?

"Shall we go out tonight?"

RIDDLE

What can run but never walks,
has a mouth but never talks,
has a head but never weeps,
has a bed but never sleeps?

A river!

Planes, Trains, & Unicycles

What do you get if you cross an Egyptian mummy with a car mechanic?

Toot and car man!

Customer: There's something wrong with my car. It has water in the carburetor.

Mechanic: Really? Water in the carburetor? I never heard of that before – I'll have to take a look at it. Where have you parked?

Customer: Er, in the lake!

Which famous brothers didn't invent the airplane?

The Wrong brothers!

What did the jack say to the broken-down car?

"Can I give you a lift?"

What kind of vehicle needs a scare?

A hiccup truck!

hiccup! hiccup!

What does a snail do on the highway?

About 10 inches an hour!

What do you call a very polite person who builds bridges and lays roads?

A civil engineer!

How did ancient Egyptians travel?

By Pharaoh-plane!

An old lady is driving carefully along the highway, when a police car behind her indicates that she should pull over. "What have I done wrong?" she wonders. "I'm not speeding, I've got my seat belt on, and my registration's in order." The lady stops and lowers the window to speak to the officer, pointing to her ear and shaking her head to show that she can't hear very well. The policeman smiles and shouts, "I know! I'm here to tell you that your horn is stuck!"

Prank #10

FOR SALE SIGN!

You will need: A piece of paper.

This is a great prank to pull on your parents and is so simple to do. Prepare a "For Sale" sign to put in the window of their car, with a cheap price and a fake telephone number.

When you know your parents will be leaving the car for a few hours, put the sign in one of the windows and wait for them to return. They will freak out at someone trying to sell their car, especially for such a low price!

PRANK LIKE A PRO: You could prepare the "For Sale" sign on a computer to disguise your handwriting. Don't forget to delete the file afterwards, though!

What do you call a dinosaur that's crashed his car?

Tyrannosaurus wrecks!

What do you call a pretend railway?

A play station!

Why wasn't your father pleased when he bumped into an old friend?

They were both driving at the time!

Air traffic controller: What's your height and position, please?

Pilot: Well, I'm 6 feet tall, and I'm sitting front left!

ROY'S DRIVING SCHOOL

**LEARN TO DRIVE QUICKLY!
CRASH COURSES AVAILABLE**

How do you catch a train?

You follow its tracks!

What did the dinosaur say after the car crash?

"I'm-so-saurus!"

What do you call a giant in an airplane seat?

Stuck!

"It took me ages to work out how to fasten the seat belt in my son's new car, then all of a sudden, it clicked!"

How does Jack Frost travel?

By icicle!

How can birds see what's behind them?

They look in their wing mirrors!

Why did the break dancer buy a car?

He fancied going for a spin!

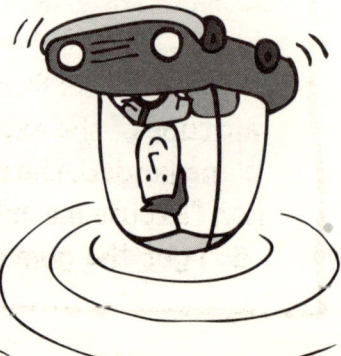

RIDDLE

If an electric train travels south, which way would the smoke go?

There wouldn't be any, it's an electric train!

Why did the farmer ride his horse to town?

It was too heavy to carry!

Which is the cleverest vehicle?

A Smart car!

An old gentleman was taking his first airplane trip. The stewardess handed him a piece of chewing gum. "It's to keep your ears from popping at high altitudes," she explained. When the plane landed, the man rushed up to her. "Excuse me, miss," he said. "How do I get the gum out of my ears?"

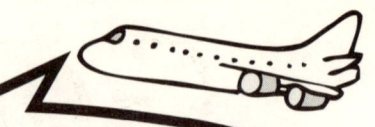

This is your pilot speaking - welcome aboard. We are pleased to have some of the best flight attendants in the industry... It's a pity none of them are on this flight!

What did the scuba diver say to the ship?

"I can see your bottom!"

What should you do with an old bike?

Recycle it.

RIDDLE

A cowboy rode to the Wild West Saloon on Friday. He stayed four nights and he left on Friday. How is this possible?

His horse was called Friday!

Goofy Gadgets

Why was the fly afraid of using the computer?

It didn't want to get tangled up in the web!

RIDDLE

What do you get after it has been taken?

A photo!

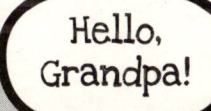

Prank #11

MOUSE TRAPPED!

You will need: A laser computer mouse.

While your victim is out, turn their computer mouse upside down and place a small piece of sticky tape over the laser.

When your victim tries to use the computer, they'll go crazy trying to figure out why it's not responding to their commands! It will take them a while to turn the mouse over and spot the prank!

PRANK LIKE A PRO: To make the prank even funnier, write "Gotcha!" on a sticky note and use this to cover the laser instead of the tape. Your victim won't fail to see the funny side!

Sam: What type of ink do we use with this printer? Black, color, or iced?

Kyle: Iced ink?

Sam: Well, now you mention it, you do a bit!

What did the computer die of?

It had a terminal illness!

How does a barber save money on his phone calls?

He cuts them short!

What did the computer do at lunchtime?

It had a byte!

BROKEN WINDOWS
Watch out for glass fragments!

Customer: My computer doesn't work. The hard drive has crashed! What should I do?

IT Technician: Did you back up?

Customer, jumping out of his chair: Why? Is it going to explode?

What is the cheapest time to call your friends long distance?

When they're not home!

They told me to scan my laptop for viruses!

Alice: If you spend any more time working on that laptop, your back problem will get worse.

Lily: How do you know?

Alice: I'm not sure, it's just a hunch.

What do you get if you cross a telephone with an iron?

A smooth operator!

Did you hear about the monkey that left bits of food all over the computer?

His dad went bananas!

What do computer operators like to eat?

Chips!

Why was the thirsty alien hanging around the computer?

He was looking for the space bar!

Hi Dad. Windows frozen! :-(

Pour some lukewarm water over them.

Er, computer completely dead now!

What takeout meal did the TV order from the restaurant?

A satellite dish!

Where can you find Spider-Man's home page?

On the world wide web!

Why do beavers spend a fortune on the internet?

They never want to log off!

Did you hear about the two antennae that got married?

They had a great reception!

Medical Madness

> **RIDDLE**
>
> What is as light as a feather, but you can't hold it for more than a few minutes, not even if you were the strongest man on Earth?
>
> Your breath!

"Doctor, doctor, I've swallowed a clock."
"Well, there's no cause for alarm!"

"Doctor, doctor, I smell like a fish."
"Oh, you poor sole!"

> **Doctor, doctor, can I get a second opinion?**
>
> **Absolutely, come back tomorrow!**

Doctor: Nurse, how is the little girl who swallowed a $1 coin last night?

Nurse: No change yet!

"Doctor, doctor, I've only got fifty seconds to live."

"Hang on. I'll be with you in a minute!"

"Doctor, doctor, I feel like a wasp."

"Buzz off! Can't you see I'm busy?"

Prank #12

THE BIG ITCH!

You will need: An old toothbrush and a T-shirt belonging to your victim.

Cut the soft bristles of an old toothbrush into tiny pieces.

Take a T-shirt from your victim's drawer and turn it inside out. Sprinkle a few bristles on the inside of the T-shirt and place it back where you found it.

When your victim gets dressed, they'll start complaining about the terrible itch they have!

PRANK LIKE A PRO: Make sure you don't actually press the bristles into the material. For added drama, you could start scratching as well, pretending to have the same "allergy."

"Doctor, doctor, everybody thinks I'm a liar."

"Oh, come on. I find that hard to believe!"

"Doctor, doctor, I have purple spots at the back of my throat."

"OK. Go next door and stick out your tongue."

"Will that help?"

"No, but I can't stand the other doctor!"

Prisoner: Look here, doctor! You've already removed my spleen, tonsils, adenoids, and one of my kidneys. I only came to see if you could get me out of this place!

Doctor: I am, bit by bit!

A man tells the doctor that his wife is going deaf. "Stand a little way from her and ask her a question," the doctor suggests. "If she doesn't answer, move closer and ask again. Keep going and you'll know how hard of hearing she really is." The man goes home and asks, "Honey, what's for dinner?" He doesn't hear an answer, so he moves closer and repeats the question several times until he's next to her. Finally, she answers. "For the eleventh time, I said we're having BEEF STEW!"

"Doctor, doctor, I feel like a piano."

"Sit down while I make some notes!"

What do you call a dentist who doesn't like tea?

Denis!

"Doctor, doctor, I've got strawberries growing out of my elbow."

"Oh, I've got some cream for that!"

Doctor, what does the X-ray of my head show?

Absolutely nothing!

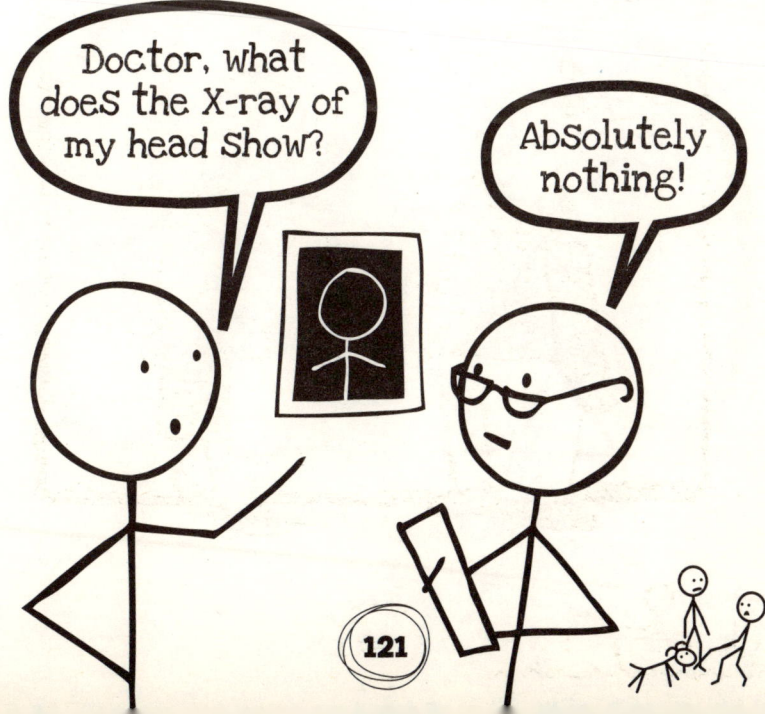

Doctor: Nurse, did you take the patient's temperature?

Nurse: No. Is it missing?

"Doctor, doctor, I feel like an apple."

"We must get to the core of this!"

Looks like your athlete's foot has returned!

Patient: Doctor, do you have a cure for sleepwalking?

Doctor: Sure, sprinkle thumbtacks around your bed!

"Doctor, doctor, I keep on getting shooting pains in my eyes when I drink tea."

"Have you tried taking the spoon out?"

Why did the banana go to the doctor?

Because it wasn't peeling well!

Patient: Doctor, I think I've swallowed a pillow.

Doctor: How do you feel?

Patient: A little down in the mouth!

"Doctor, doctor, I think I'm invisible."

"I'm sorry, I can't see you now!"

What do you call a dentist's office?

A filling station!

RIDDLE

What goes up and down but doesn't move?

Your temperature!

Patient: Doctor, doctor, I'm having trouble breathing.

Doctor: I'll soon put a stop to that.

"Doctor, doctor, I feel like a dog."

"Sit!"

Patient: How much will it cost to have this tooth taken out?

Dentist: $150.

Patient: Really?! $150 for just a few minutes' work?

Dentist: Well, I can extract it very slowly if you like!

"Doctor, doctor, you've got to help me out."

"Certainly. Which way did you come in?"

What do you call an old dentist?

Long in the tooth!

Why did the prince go to the dentist?

To get crowned!

Did you hear about the judge who went to the dentist?

He asked him to extract the tooth, the whole tooth, and nothing but the tooth!

What does a dentist do on a roller-coaster?

He braces himself!

Monstrously Funny

"Mommy, why are people scared of vampires?"

"Shh, darling. Eat your soup before it clots!"

When do ghosts normally appear?

Just before someone screams!

What is Dracula's favorite hot drink?

Decoffinated coffee!

Why did the one-eyed monster have to close his school?

He only had one pupil!

Why did the ghost starch her sheet?

So she could scare everyone stiff!

Which hairstyle do monsters like?

Deadlocks!

Who works in a monster hospital?

Skeleton staff!

What do you call two witches that live together?

Broommates!

What do you call a skeleton snake?

A rattler!

Argh, there's a hair in my soup!

Who did the ghost invite to his party?

Anyone he could dig up!

What type of art do skeletons like?

Skulltures!

What did the daddy ghost say to his family when driving?

"Fasten your sheet belt!"

What do you call a ghostly bear?

Winnie the Ooooooooooo!

What do you call a motorbike that belongs to a witch?

A brrrooooommmm stick!

Why can't skeletons play music in church?

Because they have no organs!

What did one witch say to the other witch when she was asked for a ride?

"There's always broom for one more!"

What did the ghost teacher say to his class?

"Watch the board and I'll go through it again!"

Why did the twin witches wear name tags?

So you could tell which witch was which!

What does the metal monster want written on his gravestone?

Rust in Peace!

"You don't fool me! I can see right through you!"

How do ghosts make a milkshake?

They sneak up behind a cow and yell "Boo!"

Why was the Egyptian boy upset?

His daddy was a mummy!

Why did the vampire's wife complain so much?

Her husband was a pain in the neck!

During which age did mummies live?

The band-age!

Where do ghosts go on vacation?

Death Valley!

How many zombies make a stink?

A phew!

What do shortsighted ghosts wear?

Spooktacles!

"Wake up, lazy bones!"

What do you do if you see a skeleton running across the road?

Jump out of your skin and join him!

How did the doctor bring the ghost back to life?

He took it to the living room!

Why did the mummy have no friends?

He was too wrapped up in himself!

Why are skeletons so calm?

Because nothing gets under their skin!

What do little ghosts drink?

Evaporated milk!

Why is the letter "V" like a monster?

It comes after "U"!

What does a monster mummy say to her children at lunch?

"Don't speak with someone in your mouth!"

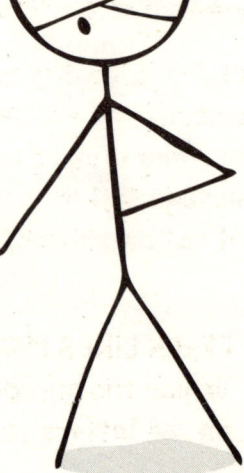

Prank #13

HAUNTED ROOM!

You will need: A bathroom with a mirror and shower, a cotton ball, and a small bowl of lemon juice.

Dip the cotton ball into the bowl and squeeze out the excess juice so that it won't drip.

With the wet cotton ball write a short scary message on the mirror. You could write "THIS ROOM IS HAUNTED" or simply "BOO!"

Let the juice dry and wait until someone takes a shower. When the room steams up, the ghostly message will appear. A scream will follow shortly afterwards!

PRANK LIKE A PRO: Make sure the juice is really dry on the mirror. To check the effect, breathe on the letters to see them appear as if by magic.

Lunar Laughs

Why do astronauts like subtractions?

They are always ready to countdown!

What's the main use for flying saucers?

To hold flying cups!

RIDDLE

I only work when I am fired. What am I?

A rocket!

What do you call a wizard from outer space?

A flying sorcerer!

Why did the boy become an astronaut?

Because he was no earthly good!

Two astronauts were in a spaceship circling high above the Earth. One had to go on a spacewalk while the other stayed inside. When the spacewalker tried to get back inside the spaceship, he discovered that the cabin door was locked, so he knocked. There was no answer. He knocked again, louder this time. There was still no answer. Finally he hammered at the door as hard as he could and heard a voice from inside the spaceship saying, "Who's there?"

What do you do if you see a spaceman?

Park in it, man!

What did the alien say when he was out of room?

I'm all spaced out!

Why don't astronauts get on well with other people?

They are not always down-to-earth!

What do aliens do when they're bored?

Play astronauts and crosses!

What did the astronaut see on the stove?

An identified frying object!

What did E.T.'s parents ask him when he got home?

"Where on Earth have you been?"

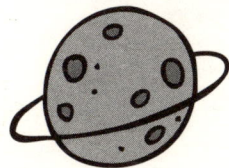

Why do aliens make crop circles?

Because they are corny!

Why did Mickey Mouse go to space?

To visit Pluto!

How do you send a baby astronaut to sleep?

You rock-et!

What type of poetry do astronauts write in space?

Uni-verses!

What does an astronaut do when he gets angry?

He blasts off!

How do you ask directions in space?

Ask-eroid!

Living on Earth is expensive, but you do get a free trip around the Sun every year!

"I told you we were flying too low!"

What goes in one year and out the other?

A time machine!

How do you know that the moon and the Earth are good friends?

They have been going around together for years!

How many astronomers does it take to change a lightbulb?

None – astronomers aren't afraid of the dark!

What holds the moon up?

Moonbeams!

OOPS!

Why don't astronauts keep their jobs very long?

Because as soon as they start, they get fired!

Did you hear about the cow astronaut?

He landed on the moooooon!

What do you get if you cross a student with an alien?

Something from another universe-ity!

What do you call an alien spaceship that drips water?

A crying saucer!

Why are astronauts successful people?

Because they always go up in the world!

What do you call a loony spaceman?

An astro-nut!

What do astronauts wear to keep warm?

Apollo neck sweaters!

Why didn't the astronauts stay on the moon?

Because it was a full moon and there was no room!

Where does an astronaut park his spaceship?

At a parking meteor!

What do you get if you cross an alien and a hot drink?

Gravi-tea!

Can you name an astronaut's favorite game?

Moon-opoly!

Last night, as I laid in bed looking at the stars, I thought to myself... "Where's the ceiling?!"